AFTER THE LOVE HAS GONE:

SURVIVING THE 8 STAGES OF A DIVORCE STORM

DWANESE E LOVE

8Love Publishing LLC

After The Love Has Gone: Surviving the 8 Stages a Divorce Storm Copyright © 2016 by Dwanese E Love
Published by 8Love Publishing LLC

All rights reserved. No part of this work may be reproduced, transmitted, stored in any form whatsoever, printed, electronically downloaded, photocopied, recorded by information storage and/or retrieval system, or individual without the prior written permission of the author.

Cover designed by Dwanese E. Love of GA
Photography by Brittany Morgan
Editing by J. Z. Alex Editing Service and Brittany S. Morgan

ISBN: 978-0-9981368-6-8
Library of Congress Control Number: 2016915783

Printed and Bound in the United States of America

To my Mom, Dad, and
Children, Brittany, Briona, Darius Jr and Demeko.
You make everything I do worth it.

I love you and thank you!

CONTENTS

Acknowledgements	6
Foreword	7
Introduction	9
Definition of a Storm	10
The Brewing Storm	11
The High Winds and Rain	20
The Impact	30
The Calm	42
The Destruction	52
The Aftermath	62
The Clean Up	75
The Next One	89
Help and Encouragement	99

ACKNOWLEDGMENTS

First, I give honor and thanks to You, Father God. It's with Your help, I made it through. Your love and this experience made me a better servant, mother, daughter, sister, friend and a better person.

To my children, Brittany, Briona, Darius Jr, Demeko, and cousin Rondell, I love you so much words cannot express. I am grateful for your support, love and yes, even your friendship through this storm. To my mother, Linda and father, Oree Jr, my heart will forever be indebted to you. I can never repay you two for what you do for us. You are truly a blessing to our entire family and I thank you from my heart. To my cousins, Chanelle and Lakenya, thank you! You wiped away my tears and showed me love when I had no strength to do so myself. Thank you and I love you both so much.

To my team of sisters from another family and my "Trues," Alania Osbourne, Monique Strachan-Murray, Juva Threat Alexander, Sacoia Anderson, Rochelle Russell, Valery George and Pamela Jones of North Dakota, I could not have gotten through this without you. I appreciate your prayers and intercessions, comforting, encouraging and even your swift kicks when I needed it. I thank God for you and cannot imagine life without you ladies. Thanks to others who were there during these dark moments. I am very grateful. Finally, I thank my ex-husband, Darius for the great years spent, our children and the lessons learned through our time together and eventually apart. May God continue to bless you.

FOREWORD

I've had the absolute pleasure of being best friends with Dwanese E. Love for over 30 years. I was there when she met her ex-husband as a teenager and was thrilled when they married and built a beautiful family together. I, just like many others felt this relationship would last forever.

The day I realized something was drastically wrong was like a shock to my system. I didn't know what to do other than to be by my friend's side and be as supportive as possible. I had no soothing words of comfort and it felt as if I was watching my friend die. I mean really, what could I say to her?

Although as a woman, I've experienced my own share of heartbreaks and break-ups, but never on this magnitude. I watched my friend at her lowest. That smile that always lit up the room was now dull. She was a shell of herself and I was so afraid. I didn't know what to do to help her other than to pray, so that's exactly what I did.

Slowly I watched her go through each of the eight stages of the divorce storm as she's so beautifully written. I'm in awe at how she's used the most painful time in her life to become a remarkable tool of healing for others. My exact words to her were, "Girl, this is NOT like any self-help book I've ever read." It is truly an action plan for those dealing with divorce, break-ups or simply have lost themselves along the way of life's journey and storms.

This book you're holding is an answer to my prayers. I didn't know how to help my friend. I didn't have the words, but God Himself, allowed her to share her heart and healed her in the process. May He use this book to bring healing to you too.

Juva Threat Alexander, Author of _From the Pole... To the Pulpit_

"After the Love Has Gone" is riveting for such a time as this! Have you given your all to ensure everything which was needed by your spouse was provided for? Are you the one who gave your last to meet their needs? Did you disregard the visions and dreams within so they could fulfill theirs? Have you denied LOVING yourself to LOVE someone who doesn't understand the meaning of true LOVE? If you answered YES to one or more of the above and have found yourself alone with more questions than answers, this is a must read for you.

Dwanese takes you through the journey and process of her personal experience of divorce. She shares in a transparent and authentic way the realities and emotions one goes through and how devastating it can be if you try to weather the storm alone. Her resilience to endure and overcome makes her a survivor; one who is fully capable of journeying with others during any stage you may be facing at the time of reading this book.

Often in life we try to hold on to what's familiar for fear of losing in the eyes of self and others, but it's in trusting as we go through the storms we discover LOVE never left, but a new level is unveiled "Self-Love." With every approaching storm in life preparation is recommended, Dwanese E Love shares <u>After the Love Has Gone: "Surviving The 8 Stages of A Divorce Storm</u> so you too may overcome.

Monique Strachan-Murray, Author of *The Soldier of Love*

INTRODUCTION

Are you searching for ways to get over the pain from an unwanted divorce? Are you dealing with rejection and self-esteem issues but are too afraid to admit it for the sake of appearing weak? Do you want to but have a hard time accepting your divorce? Tired of being told to just let go? Want to understand how?

After The Love Has Gone, Surviving the 8 Stages of a Divorce Storm, is your answer. This book will help you cope with your loss. It will offer emotional support as you go through the various stages of your divorce. The book guides you through releasing the hurt and discovering self-love.

On my journey, I encountered people going through divorce but no one offered solutions of how they survived. Hurting women and men that expressed their pain and felt the same hopelessness as I, surrounded me. When I embarked on what appeared to be answers, I was to meet with the "toughen up and get over it" spill. There was little that showed how.

I understand having unanswered questions about surviving the pain of divorce. You want to overcome the heartbreak of divorce and rediscover your happiness. I can relate. For those of you who seek real answers from someone who was rejected and survived the devastation divorce brings, this book is for you.

If you are tired of cliché written material telling you it will be ok, pick up this book and allow me to walk through this storm with you. I will help you understand the unexplainable feelings you are having. This book will equip you with strategies to regain your power, get re-acquainted with yourself and overcome the challenges of your divorce. Let's get started now!

DEFINITION OF A STORM

A violent disturbance of the normal conditions of the atmosphere, manifesting itself by winds of extreme force or direction, and often accompanied by rain, hail, thunder and lightning.

They cried out to the Lord in their trouble, And He brought them out of their distresses. He silenced the storm to a gentle whisper, So that the waves of the sea were still. Then they were glad because of the calm, And He guided them to their desired haven. ~ Psalm 107: 28-30

THE BREWING STORM

You can sense when a storm is approaching. The signs set the stage. As the storm prepares for its grand entrance, it guards its secret of what it intends to do when it arrives. Still the signs are undeniable and its arrival inevitable. The air turns colder; the wind rises from a whisper to a roaring shout, and the sun leaves the bright sky flipping the switch to black. Then the storm emerges with its sinister grin and plans to rip apart anything in its way.

Everyone received warning of a brewing storm and its predicted path. "Get your non-perishable foods, make sure you have flashlights and batteries, stock up on your water supply and board up your windows. It going to be rough," warns the weather man. "Pray that your house is still standing after the storm", he adds to himself.

The trackers cling to the advice because they understand the value of preparation. Idlers refuse to leave or prepare. They dismiss the sign the storm will be as bad. Others become careless and pay no attention to the threats at all. They embrace this moment as a time to party, slack off or ride the waves. Still the naive are clueless. They do not understand what is travelling their way. For whatever reason, they did not get the information that could save their lives. This is how people react to land storms. Similarly, this is how individuals react to storms that wipe out relationships.

If asked did they sense the end of their marriages, some individuals admit they saw signs. Alarmingly, the majority would say no. They never saw this outcome. But like a land storm, there are multiple warnings couples either ignored or took for granted. Some may have had deep-rooted beliefs divorce would not or could not happen to them.

Think about it. Every unresolved fight gave birth to the silent treatment and many nights in bed with their backs turned to each other, tear-soaked pillows and broken hearts. Raised voices turned up a notch to screaming matches. Spewing out hurtful, cut-throat words that pierced the heart became the goal. It was more important to prove who was wrong, instead of how to fix the problem. While the couple may have felt they won the battle, they were losing the war. Each saw the other as the enemy. But, the real enemy observed on the sidelines as they destroyed one another.

No one plans to divorce. However, most couples fail to prepare for the unescapable storms that arrives in marriages. People expect to live in the romantic phase of a relationship forever. They live ignorant of what it takes to withstand the brutal forces that eventually attacks all marriages. They live in denial of the problems from onset. Couples believe the problems will go away and their marriage will be untouched. They naively think it will get better. As if scripted, you will hear most justify, "All couples fight, right"?

I know this to be true because I have lived it. I am guilty of some of those things mentioned. Prior to the storm that hit my marriage, no one could have told me I would end up on the other side, divorced. We had our ups and downs but always came out unscathed from our many battles. So I thought. But no one going through attacks in their marriage comes out untouched by it. Someone and something is being hurt. Each attack left our marriage broken. It took away something with it every time. What was once beautiful and exciting became ugly and cold. Divorce resulted from many battles loss but I will tell you how I won the war.

The storm was an unwelcomed foe in the beginning. Who in their right mind want to experience the shame, fear and rejection of a failed marriage? Who signs up for feeling unloved? Did I raise my hand to be dumped after giving up the majority of my life to someone? I sure did not. There was no fine print on the marriage license that said this was part of the deal. I was confused. The storm blew fiercely and its plan destructive. But something at work bigger than the situation I had succumbed to existed. Later, I would embrace the purpose for this storm.

Nothing happens by chance and I believe everything has a reason for showing up in our lives. There are many warnings and lessons we fail to pay attention to or learn. Sometimes we are so wrapped up in our comforter of denial. However, until snatched away from us and exposing our nakedness, we even take notice to what is wrong and needs to change.

Maybe your marriage has ended in separation or divorce. You may have noticed the warning signs or was blind-sided by it. You hoped it would get better or assumed that it was not your marital house that would go down in the raging storm's path. Nevertheless, it has happened and you may not understand what to do.

The bad news is the storm you are facing is a two-part deal. It is a storm of separation of your marriage and the transformation into the storm of divorce. But with the right strategy, you will overcome both.

Divorce is death. It is safe to mourn as you work towards your goals of getting past the hurt and on with your life. The burning question in your heart now is how will you get through this storm now that your marriage has been attacked. This is especially true if the divorce was unwanted and you are still grieving the loss. I am here to help you answer that question.

Just as in a hurricane, there are many stages of post-divorce you will go through. While I am sure the person who left you have their own battles, I seek to talk to those of you who are having a tough time dealing with the loss-regardless of whose fault it seems to be. My goal here is not to point fingers or create victims but to help those who seriously want to know how to overcome the hurt of divorce.

I will share my story with you, not as a victim, but as a person who was where you are now and survived a storm designed to destroy her physically, mentally, emotionally, spiritually and financially.

As I open the book of my life to you about my former marriage and divorce, become a student and absorb all I share with you. See the things I failed to realize in my former relationship, things I wished I had done differently, my short comings and personal flaws, the moments when I finally got it right, the victories I received because of the changes I made and the lessons I learned from it all. Allow my transparency to be something that will help you through such a painful time in your life. I have been where you are so I understand. I hope it will help and encourage you to know you will make it. We are in this together.

In a land storm, there are three main things that you need to survive. That is Shelter, Food and Water. I have designed each chapter to include these three things as it relates to the divorce storm you are experiencing.

The "Shelter" section of each chapter will give words of wisdom that serves as a guide and covering to advance you through each part of the storm. "Food" will serve as a positive tool to motivate and encourage you as you progress through this life-changing event. And the "Water" section are prayers to pray that will serve as your spiritual foundation in surviving the storm.

Up ahead is stage two, the HEAVY WINDS AND RAINS. It is dark and intense, but let me show you how I got through it and how you can too!

EXPERIENCE OF THE STORM

1. You are in shock.

2. It is possible you were blindsided or you may have seen the warning signs.

3. Feelings of hopelessness and numbness exists.

4. No matter how you try to keep it together, life seems to fall apart.

SHELTER-TAKE COVER

1. Give yourself time to make sense of all of this. Do not mask or feel guilty about the feelings you have. They will come in a variety. Feel and acknowledge every one of them.

2. Stay quiet and not act on emotions. No calls, emails or texts to tell your ex off for how much they have hurt you. Truth is it probably does not matter to them at this point.

3. Secure a solid team of "Trues". Trues are family members and friends you can trust to support you and stay level-headed during this crucial time of need.

4. It is okay to be a little "needy" in this phase. Lean on your "Trues". They want to help you and you have to allow them to be there for you.

5. IMMEDIATELY cut off all contact with your ex. If you have small children and must have contact, keep it to the bare minimum, short sweet and to the point. Do not make an excuse to talk about the two of you. This means cutting off access to social media, unfriending them and even blocking them. Stay off their page. This may seem drastic but it's vital to your healing.

6. Get rid of everything that reminds you of your former spouse (not the kids of course). I do not recommend getting rid of your wedding pictures but give them to someone you can trust. Later, you may be able to look at them. For now, get them far away from you.

7. Be careful not to say anything negative in front of your children about their other parent. It's ok to vent but do

so to your "Trues," (who will be impartial and allow you to vent without judging).

8. Cry your heart out. It is okay. Losing a marriage is like a death. Mourn the loss. It is part of your healing. This does not make you a wimp or weak. It makes you HUMAN.

FOOD SUPPLY

1. Things look dreadful but it will not always be like this.

2. Accepting that you are in this storm will serve to be your strength along the way.

3. It will take a spiritual connection to overcome this one. Developing a relationship with GOD is very important (at least it was for me). He will supply you with the supernatural strength your human strength cannot carry out alone. This is a time to run to Him and learn what He is trying to teach you in this storm. Though it may feel He has deserted you, He is still there. He haven't left you.

4. You are still beautiful and amazing even if someone else stopped noticing.

WATER-QUENCH YOUR SOUL

Trust has been broken. But, this is a time to trust what you may not understand. The purpose is greater than the pain you are experiencing now. Greater things WILL come in your life (if you allow it). Say this prayer:

Lord, I don't understand why this is happening but I will trust You. I will trust Your Word as stated in Jeremiah 29:11 which tells me You know the plans You have for me. They are plans to prosper me and not to harm me, plans to give me hope and a future. Even though this hurts, I trust that through my pain You will prosper me. Give me Your strength Lord because I need it so much right now. You said where I am weak You will make me strong (2 Corinthians 12:10). Keep me close and heal my broken heart. For Your Word tells me You are close to the broken hearted and You bind up their wounds (Psalm 147:3). Forgive me Lord and help me to forgive those who have hurt me because I know forgiveness will be key to moving forward in my life. Put me back together. Strengthen me and complete the work You started in me. In Jesus name, AMEN.

THE HIGH WINDS AND RAIN

I am not a weather girl nor do I study storms for a living but I recognize they can cause extreme damage to property and people. The sad thing is even with the notice of its arrival, no one expects they will be the ones suffering the loss. Everyone thinks this sort of thing happens to the other person. It reminds me of what my Dad always says, "One day you could be the other person, never take for granted that something cannot happen to you."

As it relates to my relationship, I did not contemplate I'd end up divorced. Other people got divorced but not us. Like most married couples, we argued, but I believed our love was solid enough to withstand anything that could rise against it. But, I was now "the other person". When my storm approached, it pulled no punches. Within its massive winds it gathered up my health, my finances and then my marriage. Life became a whirlwind of complete chaos and confusion.

Did I prepare for what I saw coming? Honestly, I did not. I had not boarded my windows, I had no survival kit put together or a plan of action to protect my marriage. As the winds tore apart my marital house and the flood waters of pain overtook my life, I stood in disbelief saying, "I cannot believe divorce is happening to me."

THE HIGH WINDS AND RAIN BEFORE THE DIVORCE

I spent 21 years praying for my marriage and sacrificed even more. Now he wanted out. I could tell it was as hard for him as it was for me. At first, he hesitated to leave. I saw the struggle. But what was the use of staying? The love was just not there anymore. My heart broke at the same time as his. Sure, I could have tried harder to keep him there but my love for him did not want him to stay were his heart did not want to be. Anything forced was not worth it. I had to make a choice. It was time to let go.

Maybe it was also the fact that my pride would not allow me to fight with him one last time to save our marriage. I tried too many times but nothing worked. Did I have to give up the last bit of dignity I had? I was an inch short of begging and that did not change his mind. There were no answers to fix this.

During my rain filled nights of tears and the beating winds against my heart, I desperately desired one thing-- to not stay in the pit of my pain. I agreed not to be bitter, get lost in self-pity or become a victim of what had just happened. Something surfaced through my grief. I had to fight for Dwanese.

In the past, I asked God to take me out of a storm but this time my prayer was different. I asked Him to allow me to go through it and boy did I. Nothing could prepare me for the things I faced.

I remember lying in bed as tears ran down both sides of my face. Numb and barely existing, my eyes stared at one particular spot in the corner of the ceiling that caste a slight shadow. The rhythm of the ceiling fan blades turned in sync with the cutting pain in my heart. The cycle repeated itself for months. During the day, I wore the mask of perfection. But the night waited for me. It reminded me there was more of this storm to come.

THE HIGH WINDS AND RAIN AFTER THE DIVORCE

In this heavy winds and rains phase, I asked the "Why" questions. Why did my marriage end? Why was I not good enough for him to love? Why now, after so many years invested? My anguish lead me to question God. "God, I prayed, fasted, praised, believed and asked You to help. If

You love me, why are you allowing this?" I asked. "God if You hate divorce why did this happen to my marriage?", "God was my praying in vain?", "God did you stop loving me too", "God do you hate me?", "Are you even listening?"

I cried until I was exhausted. I searched desperately for answers I could not find. Can you relate? Are you asking these same questions?

The storm tested my faith! To make matters worse, God said nothing! At this point in my life, I can appreciate the beauty of His silence. However, when I was going through, I did NOT understand any of this.

Many times I wanted to give up. I felt unloved, unwanted, used up, dirtied up and tossed away. Not only did I feel this because of my ex's decision to stop loving me, but I assumed God felt the same way too. As crazy as this seems, I felt unloved by my Creator. The spirit of rejection was powerful! If God did not love me, I must be the blame for what was happening. But faithful is our God and I am so glad He is not like man. Softly, through the hurt, doubt and the chaos going on around me I finally heard God whisper. In the middle of the nights as I cried, He spoke His Word to my spirit, "I love you and I will never leave you or forsake you". It was a warm, soft and subtle voice. He spoke with a power my spirit eventually received. I got it!

Perhaps, you are here. You are wondering why this is happening to you. So many questions flood your mind. It does not seem real. You hurt all over. You may literally have a sting in your chest that does not seem to go away. It may hurt so much you cannot even function to do daily activities without crying. Am I right?

You cannot imagine going on without this person. It is normal. A spiritual disconnection has taken place. You have been broken. Anything broken needs time to heal. So do not let anyone make you feel guilty about hurting. My advice to you is to focus on moving forward. Fight to get through this. If not, you will remain stuck. It is safe and ok to feel the pain all while making strides forward to claim your victory!

Holding on to thoughts of reconciliation long after it is over hurts your progress. The truth is you WILL live without your ex. You must keep pushing forward.

This is where I will guide you through the inward storm you are facing now that your relationship has met its end. You may not be aware but this storm within is threatening to take away your self-worth, peace of mind, joy and your faith.

This part of the storm I compare to high winds and rain because it signifies the beginning stages of your brokenness, tears and state of confusion. In this phase, things are unclear. The winds are so strong. Your chance of survival appears slim. Just like others promised me, I too promise you will survive. You may see defeat but continue to look deeper. This journey begins the discovering of loving you and finding out what your unique design is, and it has NOTHING to do with the person who left you.

A lot takes place in this stage of the storm. You will need the proper equipment in order to make it. You may not have prepared for the storm that stole your marriage but it's not too late to prepare for the storm trying to take YOU away. Right now, your tears pour like rain and your pain increases with the intensity of the wind as you enter into the next phase. But you must continue!

We will advance to the next stage, "IMPACT". Impact has two important parts here: Recognize the impact of divorce hits hard and makes you feel as if you have lost the war. Also note that what you do during this stage of the storm has the potential to impact your future positively and bring about greatness. In the next chapter, you will discover what to do in the section of this book called IMPACT.

EXPERIENCE OF THE STORM

1. *You are heartbroken and literally sense a physical pain in your heart. You feel a "disconnect" as if a piece of you is missing.*

2. *Minutes seem longer and so does the pain. The future is something you cannot comprehend.*

3. *You do not feel you will ever be happy again.*

4. *You prayed, fasted and stood for your marriage but still ended up divorced.*

5. *You may feel God does not love you because He did not save the marriage but also because you are divorced.*

6. *Your faith is being tested. You may not feel a desire to even pray.*

7. *You feel abandoned, unloved and tossed away.*

8. *You have a lot of unanswered questions and you may even want closure.*

SHELTER - TAKE COVER

1. Make no sudden commitments or allow anyone to force you to make any long term plans about your life. This is especially true if you are separated and not yet divorced. What you have experienced is traumatic and this is no time to make hasty emotionally-based judgment calls. Things are still cloudy. Take as much time as you need to make sound choices concerning the rest of your life.

2. Be careful and analyze some of the advice you get. People that mean well will give you opinions on what they feel is best. However, it may not be best for you and your situation. Learn to trust your inner voice a little more. Even in this chaos, it will speak to you clearly. Do not go against what you recognize in your spirit is the right thing to do. For example: Have you gone against a feeling down in your core? It warned you that you should not do something. But you listened to someone's advice and did it anyway. Things fell apart or it made the situation worst. I have been there. You must trust your discerning spirit. It is a God given gift.

3. Be careful what you share, where you share and who you share it with. Realize not everybody is sad your marriage has ended. Some people may have looked forward to this day. Do not share your business with everyone. It is not for everybody. That is what your "Trues" are for. That is what God is for. By all means do not air out your dirty laundry on Facebook, Twitter, or any type of social media. It does not change the situation. It will not make your ex-spouse come back to you by shaming them. Keep private matters private. Post in generic terms. Never post names or expose flaws of your ex. If you have children with this man or woman, anything negative could come back to hurt them. This is not just about you.

4. Test your motives before you say or do anything. Ask yourself why should you do it? Is it the right thing to do? Or are you acting out of your emotions?

5. Do not keep children away from their other parent out of your pain. You are only hurting them. Their identity is connected to both of you. Do your best to encourage a healthy relationship between your ex and the children. If the other parent chooses not to see them, let that rest with them, not you. This shows the strength of your character even if the other person does not.

6. Clean yourself up. Do not stay in the dusty pajamas (or whatever your mourning clothes are) too long. Take the time to get cleaned up. Buy some good smelling lotions and bath gels. Get some fresh air! You have to keep moving forward!

FOOD SUPPLY

1. You are not damaged goods. You did not lose your worth because you lost a relationship.

2. Life brings with it many surprises. But out of those adversities will emerge our "true" selves.

3. Do not be in a rush to heal. You are broken and broken things need time to heal.

4. Your marriage failed, but that does not make you a failure.

5. God's "no" to saving a bad relationship means He has a "yes" to something even better; for example your self-discovery.

6. Even in His silence, God is still there. He has not abandoned you even if someone else has walked out of your life.

7. You are not responsible for the actions of the hurt person who has hurt you.

WATER - QUENCH YOUR SOUL

Things may appear foggy and your future looks dark. When you think all is lost and can't see pass today, understand this will not destroy you. Something greater will emerge from this storm. Pray this along the journey:

Lord I know my prayers and tears were not in vain then and I know they are not in vain now. I believe You heard every prayer and saw every tear. The answer seems to be no and I trust you see and know more than I. Father, you know me and my heart even if no one else does. You know how I felt towards my marriage and the sacredness I hold for matrimony. Lord, You missed nothing and saw everything. You saw what was done by both parties. I believe you would withhold nothing good from me. I realize you did not cause my marriage to end but have an important reason for allowing it to do so. For this I must pay close attention. Show me what you want me to know and the lessons I must learn from this. Advance me to the next level. Be my shelter from this hurricane, cover my exposed wounds and bring comfort to my spirit. Use my pain for your glory and equip me with what I need as you bring me through this storm. Place my feet on dry land. A land filled with your rewards, blessings and favor. I cannot do this alone but with you and the strength you give, I can do all things. Thank you for being here with me, especially when I feel alone. Thank you for the great things waiting for me. In Jesus name. Amen.

THE IMPACT

When buying our first house, I do not know how I overlooked that gigantic fir tree on the upper right corner of the front yard. This thing appeared to shoot up 100 feet in the air. The tree stood tall, strong and unmovable like a giant Christmas tree on steroids.

This tree was a reminder of the uneasiness I felt. If hit by a major hurricane, the damage would be huge! I wanted the tree gone. But the price to remove the tree was more than our budget allowed. The problem was later solved. The tree became our symbol of the power of a storm.

For the most part, our area never got hit hard. But, I still took precautions and evacuated to make sure my family and I were out of harm's way. Safety made sense compared to being caught in the storm's wrath.

The hurricanes in the year 2005 repeatedly called our bluff. I grew tired of the warnings of a ferocious storm threating to take down South Florida. I soon refused to give attention to the weather man's warning of storms headed our way. One of those storms broke a single tree branch in our yard that laid in our driveway as a reminder of how *vicious* it was. Traveling was becoming expensive and exhausting. It no longer made sense to leave our home for what appeared to be false predictions.

 I took the normal precautions and stayed home. My family and I would ride this one out. Even though Katrina had just devastated New Orleans, her "baby sister" was not going to have that kind of impact on us. It was not historically correct. Besides, we had already had too many false alarms to count. I was convinced Fort Lauderdale was safe.

Hurricane Wilma was her name. She had us South Floridians laughing and waiting for her to come and grace us with her presence and leave because we had beach living to do. But ole Wilma had plans of her own.

Crazy enough out of some insane curiosity, my family and I opened our front door to see what a storm looks like when it hits land. We heard the infamous loud train whistle others warned about. We joked of that tree falling in the streets on the corner not harming anyone else's house. The joke later gave way to serious thought of that idea. We huddled up and prayed for the fir tree to fall just like we asked. And Wilma graciously obliged. A loud crack and the tree crashed in the road not touching any of the four houses on our corner. It was a miracle! We cheered and continued to watch her performance.

We watch Wilma do her thing as she commanded our attention. Her impact was of strength and fierceness. She almost gained my respect as I witnessed her peel back a few shingles off of rooftops and whip a few leaves and branches off of the trees. This was not so bad. But we underestimated her impact just like most of us do when hit by something so devastating in our lives.

During the beginning of the storm, Hurricane Wilma's impact did not appear to do much damage, at least nothing we could not handle, even in her midst. But there was more to come and we were not prepared.

THE IMPACT BEFORE THE DIVORCE

My heart breaks when someone's marriage and family is destroyed. The damage is unsurmountable. I remember the announcement to our kids when I told them their dad and I were separating. Knowing the household our family had made this one of the hardest things to do.

My house was always noisy, and I loved it! Either you heard my children downstairs cracking jokes on one another or critiquing every movie they watched. Born movie critics that held nothing back. This sealed their strong bond. My eyes watered and I laughed hysterically at the stuff they said. My house was a home I looked forward to at the end of a long day. It was filled with so much laughter and joy, but that would soon end.

I recall how icy our house felt after the realization our family was splitting apart. Everyone exited to their own separate rooms. The laughter stopped and all that could be heard was an emotionless silence and our new house guest, "Division". Division became the new owner and was certainly in charge.

It seemed the enemy won the very thing I fought so hard to keep together. I thought I had hit him hard because we overcame a lot through the years. However, his impact was even harder. He had my family in the palm of his hand and I envisioned him laughing saying, "See your prayers did not work after all." I felt defeated.

The divorce followed two years later. For so long, I vowed never to file divorce papers. That was against my spiritual belief. If anyone should bare that burden it should be him. But as the situation progressed and new circumstances developed, I finally filed for divorce against everything I stood for.

THE IMPACT AFTER THE DIVORCE

I started to feel good again. Still hurting but I knew I was going to live. I made the decision to go through with the divorce. Then, one of my Trues came up with an idea to throw a party. At first this did not seem like a good idea. Besides, I did not want to celebrate getting a divorce. What she proposed was different. Since I had overcome so much, it was a suggested rite of passage to celebrate my accomplishments. That was a fresh look at it and the event planner in me ran with the opportunity. Hence the "Freedom Party" was born.

It was not like the divorce parties that got wild or bash the ex. It represented freedom on so many levels. From the beginning, I strived for freedom. This was not about him at all. It was a true celebration of ME! The "me" that overcame and soon to be discovered.

The Freedom Party gave me the chance to express appreciation for each of the women that had been there for me. I made sure the party had surprises that reflected my gratitude towards them. I was so happy that night. Each of my friends spoke prophetic words over me and celebrated my new beginning. Yes, I was getting a divorce but that did not mean it was the end of my life. I survived the separation! I was going to survive the divorce too! But the impact of the storm was far from over.

Two weeks later the papers came in the mail stating the divorce was final. I was numb and not sure how to feel. I wanted to be happy. Losing the progress I made was not an option. I had come too far. But no matter how much I forced happiness I could not find it. Memories of when we first met, our high school years together, our first time, our wedding day, the birth of our kids, the pillow fights came rushing in like a flood and I could not turn it off. I needed to turn it off! This was my life now! There was no room for what was. Instantly, I was broken again, as if he had just walked out.

For the next few days, I pushed my family and friends away. I ignored their calls and did not go out. Locked in my room, I dwelled in my pain. I could let no one see me like this. They had invested so much time and energy in helping me. There was no way I would ask them to do this all over again. The more isolated I became the more the enemy played with my mind. This was his strategy to take me out. He was trying to tell me that no one loved me and not to trust anybody. The devil mocked and reminded me of "my love-and-once-best-friend's" betrayal. How could I trust anyone else? I felt alone. But I soon realized I was not as alone as I wanted to be. God was still there. I prayed real hard and sought Him more. He said isolation was not the answer. He told me to tell my family and friends what was happening. So I did. And guess what? They understood and went even harder for me. I am in tears as I write this. Love is a powerful thing but we have to learn to accept it. The impact of the love I received counteracted everything the enemy threw at me and it superseded the love I thought I had lost.

I learned isolation is only ok if you are diligently seeking God and not to remove people out of your life. We need one another. I learned that transparency is key. While you do not share your business with just anybody, you will have to open up to those you can trust. They exist. Sometimes we do not see it because we are yearning for what we loss. During this time, develop your relationship with God. His strength will increase yours. With God and the people He places in your life, you will make it. It is important that you learn to accept the love others are trying to give to you. Do not push them away. I did that. But I am so glad I learned to accept being loved from people willing to genuinely and freely give it. That was difficult but freeing.

I remember desperately searching for a divorce support group and other resources, but help was limited or conflicted with my work schedule. Looking back, God did this on purpose because He wanted me to depend solely on Him for the majority of my healing. It amazes me how the resources became plentiful AFTER the experience of the storm.

It did not stop my quest to seek help. I joined a group I thought was for divorced women. Instead, I was in the midst of women who were married 20, 30 even 40 years. God has such a sense of humor, right? I was shocked because God did not give me the support from a local divorce support group. What He gave me was Him and a chance to experience every single thing I am writing for myself. It was later I encountered people in droves that experienced the storm of divorce AND made it through. It was all in His timing.

I am not saying not to seek help. In fact, I encourage it. Especially if you are in a dark place and you are having a hard time coping. Please do not neglect getting outside help. It may be of great importance to seek counseling on your journey forward to help you sort out some things.

The impact of your divorce may have hit you hard, but this is the time to fight even harder to overcome its power-pounding blows. Get back up! You may have to repeat this step but that is ok. During this phase you will get knocked down a few times. Healing is never in a sequence. It cannot be rushed. I learned this the hard way. The key is getting back up! Are you ready to get back up? Focus and get ready to receive what you need to survive the IMPACT phase of the storm located immediately at the end of this chapter. These tools will help you in the next stage. Keep in mind things may appear to get better as you move forward to the next phase called THE CALM. Don't let your guard down yet. Stay with me to understand why.

EXPERIENCE OF THE STORM

1. You may feel the finality of the end of the marriage.

2. It could take a toll on your children and they may act out or withdraw.

3. You may make progress forward just to go two steps backwards.

4. You may not be as over it as you want to be.

5. You feel betrayed and trust no one.

6. You may suffer from a mild depression.

7. It is a normal reaction to want to push everyone away and isolate yourself as means to guard yourself from further hurt; especially towards those who care about you.

8. You feel defeated as if the devil won. (The devil is a liar! Had to interject that.)

SHELTER-TAKE COVER

1. FORGIVE! This can't be negotiated! Forgiveness is more about you than you realize. It is what I call a "Selfless-Selfish" act. Forgiving the other person does not let them off the hook, but it releases your control to punish them. It is selfless because it removes "self" out of the picture. It frees you and gives God the right to be judge and jury as it should be. It's "selfish" (in a positive way) because when you forgive, it opens the door to your many blessings and rewards that are forfeited if you chose not to forgive. Makes sense? Keep in mind, we have been on the other side of hurting someone and they have forgiven us. God forgave us for sins we still commit against him. For the times you desired forgiveness, how would you have felt if you had not gotten it? I know this is difficult especially if you have been hurt badly. Remember, I have been there. It is difficult, but doable. Forgiving may feel "against the grain" and not normal. But, it's in the difficult things we do that allows us to defeat the enemy.

2. Bond more with your children. They need you and you need them. Let them express how they feel about all of this. Listen to what they have to say without your input or judgment. This is not just about the two of you. This is difficult for them too.

3. Be mindful of the things you do. It can have a long term effect on those you love. Divorce impacts not just you; it impacts your children, your family, your ex-spouse's family, your mutual friends and others who may have followed your marriage and was sadden by its lost. Often our marriages serve to inspire people we have no clue are watching. Marriage is a ministry and the enemy's main target.

4. It is ok to seek help. If you are finding it hard coping, find a qualified counselor in your church or join a local (or online) divorce support group. If you feel or show signs of depression, get help IMMEDIATELY!

5. Do not isolate yourself from the people who love and support you. Putting your guard down and allowing love in is something your soul needs. Do not deny yourself the love from those who really and truly love you. Opening up and trusting is your ticket to healing. Do not let someone who broke your trust cause you to miss out on new opportunities to build lasting and solid relationships with people who genuinely love you.

6. Protect your mind. There will be times when you feel you will lose your mind because you are thinking too much or trying too hard to figure things out. Schedule 5-15 minute breaks. Set your timer and just relax. Say a prayer of protection over your mind. It is the enemy's access into your life. Intentionally guard your mind! Relieve stress and stop trying to figure everything out. Change what you can and accept the rest.

7. Laugh more. Rent funny movies, attend comedy shows or surround yourself with people who make you laugh. Laughter is the best medicine. It can bring relief to the gloom you have been experiencing.

8. Take a hiatus or a break to seek God. Set days to shut down your social media, refrain from text or calls to get alone with God in prayer. Make sure you are taking a hiatus to seek God and not to cut off your family and friends. In fact, let them know what you are doing and leave the door open to at least one close person to check on you regularly during your hiatus. During this time "date" God. Make dates to meet at the library, Starbucks, the park, your favorite lunch spot, etc. Take your bible, notebook and a pen. Quiet your spirit. Asked God to guide you to what He wants to talk to you about or look up

scriptures of things you are facing and need His help with. This is a time of reflection, correction and empowerment. Let God have His way.

FOOD SUPPLY

1. When you master the difficult things you defeat the enemy.

2. Forgiveness is one key to spiritual success.

3. You still serve as a positive influence on others. Keep a servant's heart and do what is right. People are watching how you handle this storm.

4. God has equipped you with the ones who are SUPPOSED to be in your life. Loved ones that adore you and value your presence in their lives.

5. There are more (quality) for you than against you. "Quality" is better than "Quantity".

6. Get knocked down seven times get back up eight! (A Japanese proverb).

WATER-QUENCH YOUR SOUL

Life can hit you so hard sometimes causing pain you never imagine experiencing. It makes you wonder how you will get up from this. You must continue the journey. Stay on the path! Do not give up! Say this prayer:

Lord, Your Word says a house divided against itself falls (Mark 3:25). My marital house has fallen, and it has left me and my family scattered and broken hearted. I know You have the power to restore what the enemy has stolen (Joel 2:25-26) Restore our joy, our peace and our love. Please let us find assurance in You despite what has happened, remembering You are in control and before long we will walk in Your real purpose for us. Let us count it all joy the trials and tribulations of this storm knowing greater things are ahead for us. (James 1:2) When things get too hard for us to handle, let us find refuge in you. Allow us to hide under Your wings. Protect us and continue to shepherd us through this storm. (Psalms 91:4) Be our eyes where we cannot see and help us to keep them on You rather than the things we are experiencing. (2 Corinthians 5:7) Open the door to divine connections. Bring us help in every area we need. Give us strength to continue on and not give up or turn back. Thank You for loving us through what seems so hard right now. Thank You that we will make it. In Jesus Name. Amen

THE CALM

Remember Hurricane Wilma and how I told you we watched her in awe. She danced her way around our neighborhood not causing much damage. Her impact may not have been so great on first contact as her predecessors but that was her plan.

After Wilma's winds had blown through a few trees (and destroyed our gigantic Christmas tree), I saw the sun slightly peak through the dark clouds. "That's all?" I asked. I was glad we stayed home.

This was not so bad and we had nothing to fear. We joked and enjoyed the now calm, cool winds of the morning that came with Wilma's coy behavior. We did not appreciate the inconvenience of the storm, but we were surviving it.

Then stories from my older relatives came to mind. They shared their accounts of when Hurricane Betsy struck Louisiana back in September 1965. "The calm before the storm," they reported. I was about to learn personally what they meant.

THE CALM BEFORE THE DIVORCE

How many times did your marriage survive a fight? It looked bad, but you endured. Things worked out, so you continued making plans for your future.

Your relationship survived hurtful words, abuse or infidelities. Maybe months or even years passed with no more drama. You felt safe. Hey, you made it through the debris that life had thrown your way. You thought nothing would tear you apart… until finally it did!

It was that way for me. We overcame so much and promised we were not going anywhere. Convinced, we were in it to win it. We were too comfortable thinking nothing could separate us. Besides, we were too strong to let that happen. But life had another agenda our false strength was no match for. Like that strong, tall tree, our marriage came plummeting down!

THE CALM AFTER THE DIVORCE

Time passed, and I was happy again. The pain lessened, and I did not wake up as often in tears or dream about him. I did more. Buying a new outfit was one of my small victories. I visited my cousins in Louisiana and my best friend in Florida. I ate out with my friends and enjoyed movie nights with my children. My dark life was looking brighter.

He was going on with his life. Now I was going on with mine. As the days continued, living without him got easier. Besides, I was fed up with living in the pit. I welcomed anything that resembled joy.

Even being friends with my ex was ok now. I still loved him but accepted that our roles had changed. There were mixed messages sometimes on both our parts but I always tried to keep it cordial versus fantasizing of us reconciling. Our friendship seemed right, but was it?

The "Calm" phase of the storm can fool us if we are not careful. This is the stage of "DO NOT's" we must adhere to. I have included them at the end of this chapter. It's possible to miss them because we think we have finally arrived. We open ourselves up to things we say we would never do. Why? Because we are still emotionally wounded. Our desire to be over the hurt causes us to be blinded by the truth.

Everything looks great, but it's an illusion. Positive things are happening for you. The sun is shining on your life and these are the feelings you are desperately clinging to. The rains have stopped and the winds are calmer but the storm is not finished. You do not want go back to being sad or hurt. But you cannot afford to ignore the smoke screen. You are in the eye of the storm!

Your mind believes you are healed, but the truth is you are not. The storm has to run its course. That will require more learning and healing. Whether you accept it or not, the storm must fulfill its intended purpose.

In the calm of the storm, briefly enjoy the moment but stand guard for what is to come. I know you are saying, "Oh Lord, there's more? I can't handle any more disappointments"! But remember what James 1:4 says, "Let patience have her perfect work that you may be perfect and complete wanting nothing"! This storm came to accomplish that work.

The experience does not have to be painful. But, it holds lessons you will need to overcome this entity. This is a time of inspection and reflection. Inspection of self. It is where you analyze the point where you started from to where you are now in your life. The Calm phase is where you review what you have learned so far to take you through the rest of the storm.

Avoid getting into a new relationship right now. Take the time to work on you. I REPEAT, THIS IS NO TIME FOR A NEW RELATIONSHIP! Instead, this is the perfect time to develop a relationship with YOURSELF. See where you went wrong. Evaluate the part you played in the demise of your marriage and what you will do better next time. Get rid of false beliefs about yourself and incorporate healthier, positive ways in which you see yourself. Fail to do this now and I promise you the battle will be far from over. I learned the hard way so I can attest to that.

Mistakes in this phase can cost you the progress you made. This mishap can prevent you from learning the lessons this storm comes to teach. You will stumble a few times in the healing process, however, your goal is not to stay in the same phase. It is important you progress to the stage of acceptance so you can move on with your life. Slow down and focus. Do the necessary work to get you through this refreshed, renewed and restored.

In the calm of a land storm, the sun may come out. And if there is no real evidence of devastation, it can fool you. The sunshine may tempt you to go for a ride or do anything to get back to living. We know this would not be smart because the storm is not over.

It's also true with a life storm. You cannot be in a rush to go on as if nothing happened. The storm has showed up for a reason and it serves you best to pay close attention to what that reason is. Endure the storm even though it does not feel good. It has to complete its cycle. You will appreciate it later.

So let's look at what you should do in THE CALM phase and the DO NOT's I talked about. I stress the storm is not finished because I want you to stay alert. You have to "boot up" for the DESTRUCTION that comes shortly after the calm of the storm. So let's continue. Our work is not done yet!

EXPERIENCE OF THE STORM

1. *Things are getting better and you are laughing more.*

2. *You are enjoying the company of others.*

3. *There is false sense of healing and you think you are ready for a new relationship.*

4. *Possibly, you are the opposite of the above and are bitter. You shun the thought of a future relationship.*

5. *You may want to foster a positive relationship or feel strong enough for open communication with your ex.*

6. *You may open yourself up to false hopes and disappointments of reconciliation with your ex or still want it.*

7. *You have the possibility to move ahead too fast opening the door for poor judgment and many mistakes.*

8. *This the time for self-reflection and review of lessons you have learned.*

SHELTER - TAKE COVER

1. Trying to ease the pain by getting into another relationship too soon may not be a good idea. It can be a disaster if you are not completely healed. You might open the door to a repeated pattern of relationships that are not good for you, hurting an innocent person because you do not love them, and experiencing another failed relationship because you simply are not ready. Do Not #1-get into a new relationship right now.

2. Avoid getting intimately involved with your ex. It does not matter how long you two were together. The fact is, he or she is no longer your husband or wife. There are mixed and raw emotions that exists. It does not mean love is still there or the other person wants you back. Tough to swallow, I know. The sooner you accept this the sooner you can move on. You are "familiar" to each other. It is easy to gravitate to what is comfortable. Being intimate brings comfort for the pain of the severing of ties (even if the fix is temporary). Doing this gives you false hopes, further rejection and delays your healing. You are only giving yourself away to someone who no longer deserves to have you. Do Not #2-sleep with your ex.

3. Brace yourself for the possibility of your ex moving on and being in love with someone else. You may not understand why they chose not to work things out with you. They may treat the other person better. Your ex has moved on. It's ok to do the same! Do Not #3-hold on to false hopes of reconciliation.

4. The calm of the storm is a time to reflect on what took place and provide a time to breathe. It is a time to focus on finding the path of relying on yourself for the love you sought from your former partner. Use this time to

see life without them. Use the pain to accept in your heart and mind it is over and that's okay. Do Not #4- forfeit your healing.

5. Those of you who are convinced you are okay with nobody in your life ever again, or the breakup did not hurt you, you maybe fooling yourself. One failed relationship does not dictate the success of a future one. Please realize you are hurting yourself by shutting out future love or pretending your spouse's leaving does not hurt you. Denial is your worst enemy. Confronting what you fear and being honest about your feelings must be priority if you are going to overcome this thing. Remember still loving your ex does not make you a fool. Pretending you do not only hurts your progress. It is okay to feel everything you are feeling. And as you progress, keep yourself open to love in your future. Do Not #5-give up on a future loving relationship or deny your pain.

6. If you are not ready to be friends with your ex, do not rush it. Nothing is written in concrete that says you have to be friends with your ex if you are not ready. Give yourself time and distance if you need that. You are only called to forgive, not be best buds with your ex. In time, once you have taken care of YOU, then you can be friends. Do Not #6- force a friendship with your ex.

7. Take comfort in God and make healing your top priority. That means putting off getting involved with another person. It also means not entertaining the thoughts of reconciliation with your ex if one-sided. Focus on YOU! You are worth it!

8. If you have made any of the mistakes mentioned during this phase, it can cause an issue later. But, do not beat

yourself up. Use this as an opportunity to learn. You will appreciate the lessons once this storm is over.

FOOD SUPPLY

1. Forgiving others and yourself does not make you weak but makes you strong.

2. You will not always get it right but learning from your mistakes will guide you through the storm to victory.

3. You may face disappointments from others but never let it stop you from loving and seeing the good in people.

4. You are more than enough!

WATER - QUENCH YOUR SOUL

When we have been overwhelmed, finally getting relief can be breathtaking. However, we can mistakenly think the problem is over. We prematurely go back to living as normal. If no real change has occurred, this is dangerous. It leaves room for mistakes. Be mindful during this time. God is not finished with you. Say this prayer:

Lord, it feels great to finally get a break from the storm. But during this time, help me not to move too fast. Help me to slow down and take inventory of what has happened. Give me a discerning spirit to acknowledge the lessons and information You are trying to get to me. Help me not to make decisions out of my pain or rely on false information the enemy may strategically send my way to throw me off track. Help me not to let my emotions or the things I desire get the best of me. Help me to be patient with this storm and allow me to see the benefits. Let me not lean to my own understanding or try to fix things the way I think they should be. Help me to trust You. Regardless, it is Your will that will be done. All will be well. Thank you for never letting me forget You are with me and You are in control. In Jesus Name. Amen.

THE DESTRUCTION

I f we underestimated Wilma before halftime we learned she was not to be played with 3rd and 4th quarter of the game. Instead of shingles, she came back cutting away roofs, knocking over power lines and uprooting trees.

We had enough of watching her show and closed the door; we were convinced of her power. Wilma did us a friendly favor by knocking down that tree without harming us or our neighbors. But, her friendship ceased and showed no mercy when she came back for our house. Wilma wanted payment for the work she had done for us.

I had seen nothing like it. I remember sitting in our dining room that opened into the living room. Suddenly, a small bubble formed in the living room ceiling. It grew bigger and bigger as if someone was chewing bubble gum and blowing an enormous bubble. It grew until it overtook the entire ceiling. We frantically moved our furniture out of the area. When we had gotten everything out of the way, the ceiling crashed! We stood in shock! I couldn't speak. The tears wouldn't flow. I stood there in disbelief. Now her job and purpose was complete. The rest was left up to us.

I was grateful my family and I were alive and unharmed. We were not sure just how much damage this storm had caused but our neighborhood was a billboard of evidence damage was done. With destruction around us, it left us pondering what were we going to do to fix the huge mess.

THE DESTRUCTION BEFORE THE DIVORCE

I can recall many instances of destruction before the divorce took place. One was the night before my birthday, the year of our separation. The fights were bad, but this one was the worst. I remember the state of haziness I felt. I was a walking corpse. Not allowed to live yet not allowed to die. The storm did not come as physical blows just emotional torture and games that hurt just the same. Why couldn't this be a normal breakup? When a man decides to leave, he leaves. He does not stick around. But that would have forfeited fates chance to wound me deeply. My self-esteem, my worth and my dignity had to be stripped away first.

He said he wanted to leave. But, it was a month now, and we still slept in the same bed. This was emotional torture. I had to do something to make him leave; but what? Should I threaten to kill myself? Or maybe I should make him think I am crazy and threaten him? That would make him leave our bed. Maybe he would leave the house and never look back.

We went in for the kill one last time. I did and said some things I am not proud of. My heart would not let me hurt him or myself. I just wanted the pain to stop. Despite the pain, I still loved this man with all of my heart. I loved our children and above all I loved my freedom. The enemy was not going to make this easy. We were over! The destruction was done. I had gotten my wish for him to leave our room. But I failed in getting him to leave our home. Two months of mental torture since his announcement before he would leave. This was too much for me to handle.

Prior to this, my health was failing. I did not want to have surgery, but it was unavoidable. I kept putting it off. No time seemed to work with his schedule and I wanted him there. But on surgery day, my children, mother, father, best friend from middle school and my cousin who flew in from out-of-state were the last faces I saw before being wheeled back for surgery. "Is that your family out there"? asked the nurse. "Yes," I said. "There is sure a whole lot of love out there for you," she replied as if to confirm I was loved. When she left the room, I cried. I recognized the love. Love was praying for me, and minutes before assuring me I would be alright. That love was waiting for me to come back to them. So why did I mourn for the love I thought would show up, but never came?

When I got home, he did not ask if I was ok. It had been a month since the fight but we were on speaking terms so I could not understand the no show or not being welcomed home. It would be unfair to condemn or explain his side or reason for his response. I am sure he was battling his own storm. I smiled in his presence to assure him I had no hard feelings but when the bedroom door was shut, I was a broken mess. The tears would not stop flowing. I lifted my head at the moment my cousin took my hand and squeezed it real tight. I saw she had tears of her own. She wiped the endless tears from my eyes, ignoring the ones in hers. "You are going to make it!" she promised. I needed to believe her. But the pain would not let me. I went to sleep that night not knowing what the next few days would bring.

"I can't breathe," I shouted out of my bathroom door right before I felt myself about to hit the floor. My cousin who had not left me since I got home from the hospital ran and helped me get dressed. I asked her to call my dad to take me to the hospital. "Don't say anything to him or the kids," I begged her. It was Memorial Day and a chance for the kids and their father to enjoy the holiday together. I did not want to ruin it for them. She reluctantly agreed. My dad showed up but too nervous to drive. My oldest daughter realized what was going on and drove me to the hospital.

When I arrived, I was convinced I would be released. Things could not get any worse than this, right? I was wrong. The doctor said I had developed blood clots from the surgery. I spent a week in the hospital wrestling with which one hurt the most, the shots from needles with medicine that burned the insides of my stomach or the heartbreak of watching the last 21 years of my life fall apart. To make matters worse, two days into my hospital stay, he packed his things and left for good.

THE DESTRUCTION AFTER THE DIVORCE

What is it that causes us to want our ex long after the love has gone? One reason is we hold on to the mind-movie of the wedding day. But the person who vowed to love us forever no longer exists. The heart tells you he (she) is still your husband (wife) but the truth is he (she) is not. You two are divorced.

Giving yourself to your ex opens the door to further rejection. It can sabotage any progress you have made coming to terms with life without marriage. I speak from experience. It is wise to allow yourself more time to heal without complicating things with sex (because it's no longer love making).

For me, it brought even more shame. But proved to be the reality check I needed. This was over! The connection felt dead and meaningless. Giving yourself to an ex does not mean reconciliation. We cannot afford to let this trip us up.

"Aren't you worth more", I asked myself. I was not a "jump off" but I played the part because of my belief he would always be my husband. My excuse? It was covenant. But though God does not break covenant, man does. Our covenant was broken long time ago. Side note: please stop fooling yourself with this one if you are doing this too. You are no longer married, no matter what you believe or feel.

Rejection from your ex is not the only kind you may experience in this phase. There will be rejection from other people. You'd think after a loss like divorce (resembling death) you would find people who are more understanding or sympathetic. Quite the opposite, some people will shun you. Mutual friends may stop talking to you. Your in-laws may not want to continue a relationship with you. Other married acquaintances may treat you different. Frankly, some folks are happy your marriage is over. How do you handle that? Simple, do not take it personally.

What I discovered is that sometimes people cannot vocalize or deal with your break up. It can be a reflection of their own troubled marriage and that can scare them.

Mutual friends and family could be sad or disappointed about your divorce. They do not want to choose sides because they love and respect both of you.

However, there are those who marked their calendars for the day of your divorce. The ones that were preparing themselves to be the next Mrs. (or Mr.) and the ink was not dry on your divorce papers yet. Don't let that intimidate you. You are the real prize!

God uses this time to uproot fakers and expose haters. We get to see clearly who is for us or who is against us. I am telling you what I know. This phase will teach you to value yourself, set boundaries and cut those ties. It is important to let God prune whoever He needs to prune out of your life. This is a blessing not a curse. Those who really love you will be there for you no matter what.

And for those who gloated about your demise, smile and let the haters do their job. Your story is not over. There is so much more for them to see. They get to watch the amazing things God is about to do for you. It is not boasting in your own strength, it's about the promise of God. Do your part to be obedient and watch Him work it out for you.

The last thing you might encounter is "guilt trippers". People who tell you that you are committing a sin if you get divorced. What do you do when the choice is not yours?

Let me free you. God is our creator and He does not force us to love or accept Him. It is in our best interest we do but He gives us "freewill." Why? Because He wants us to "genuinely" love Him; not be forced to love Him. Why should we feel entitled for Him to force someone else to love us after they have made the choice not to? Also, there is no condemnation to those who belong to Christ (Romans 8:1).

You will have to trust God in this. If it is in His plan for your life, you may experience reconciliation but do not get stuck on that. Want in your heart what God wants for you. If His answer is no, be prepared to accept that. Proverbs 19:21 says, "Many are the plans in a person's heart, but it is the Lord's purpose that will prevail". And yes even in this divorce, He has a purpose. I will keep reminding you because it is important you get it!

Everything around you looks a mess. Financially you may be in a hole and you are working harder to take care of your children. You may be raising your kids by yourself with no help or emotional support from their other parent. Your ex may have found someone else and planning a life with that person while you are trying to pick up the pieces of your own. Make the commitment to yourself you will continue to push through the false hopes, the pain, the memories and anything else that may hold you back from living the life God has planned for you. I know this storm has caused great ruin but what you do not realize is you are approaching the end. With a focused plan, you will rebuild. You will have to assess the situation in the AFTERMATH phase, before the final phase. Are you ready to do the work?

EXPERIENCE OF THE STORM

1. If you made mistakes in the "Calm" phase look for it to show up here.

2. You may have crossed the lines of intimacy with your ex and now regret it.

3. You could experience rejection from mutual friends and family members.

4. You will recognize who is for you and who is not.

5. You may have suffered a setback.

6. You may feel overwhelmed with doing everything by yourself.

7. You are crushed by the devastation.

8. This is a sign the storm is coming to its end.

SHELTER - TAKE COVER

1. Realize you cannot make someone love you. We all have a choice.

2. Be prepared for further rejection from mutual associates or family members. Do not take it personally. Some will fall off and it is ok. That is God's way of uprooting the weeds. He will reveal the hearts of people who adore you.

3. Do not take every rejection personally. Sometimes people may not know how to react and mean no harm.

4. Make rejection your best friend. The more it shows up, the less it will matter who accepts you or not.

5. You are NOT defeated no matter what it looks like.

6. Sometimes we will lose some things and people during the Divorce Storm. See these losses as a gift from God. They are signs of goodness that is about to show up.

7. God remains faithful when a man or woman is not. His faithfulness is guaranteed. You have to stay focused!

8. Do not be a victim. Your goal is to move on. There is a time to mourn a loss. But, also a time to stop rehearsing the hurt and telling that story. Your best life is waiting to be written. The question is "do you want to stay in your hurt" or "do you wish to explore a brand new life where you can be happy again"? It is really your choice.

FOOD SUPPLY

1. Lovingly let go of anyone who does not want to be in your life.

2. Knowing, loving, and accepting who you are opens the door to happiness you could have only imagined.

3. Respect yourself and know you are worthy of being loved, respected and valued.

4. Release anything that shows you otherwise.

5. Embrace pain as a signal something in your life needs to change.

6. What appears to be defeat is your scheduled victory in disguise.

7. Spend your "time bucks" wisely. Your time is golden and better spent on the ones who genuinely love you.

8. Under the rubble of this destruction is your true self. It is time you got to know her (him).

WATER - QUENCH YOUR SOUL

It may look real bad. Seems like all is lost and hopeless; You have encountered disappointment after disappointment. The heat seems intense. Remain calm. Say this prayer:

Lord, I know the enemy is betting on me to give up. He wants me to stop giving or receiving love. I pray, despite the evidence of hurt and pain that surrounds me, You increase my desire to love even more. Your Word says perfect love casts out fear. Open me up to loving without fear. Open my eyes to recognize the prized gems You have already placed in my life and the ones to come. Help me to shower them with my love and to focus more on them and not on the ones who are against me. Increase my love walk and soften my heart. Out of the rubble of pain, teach me how to love myself again and to embrace Your love for me. Give me the heart to love unconditionally and to let go (in love) those who desire to exit my life. Give me the heart to pray for those who hurt me or use me. Help me to release them into Your hands and not feel the need to take vengeance into my own. Vengeance is Yours. Help me to grow forward knowing what was set out to destroy me has no victory over me. I have already won! In Jesus Name. Amen.

THE AFTERMATH

No I am not talking about a Dr. Dre compilation album, I am talking real life chaos here. The end of a marriage can devastate but its after effects can be far more damaging on an individual than the divorce itself.

Your sense of security, peace and self-worth appears to have been destroyed. Your future looks uncertain and your faith tested to extreme confines. You have suffered a great loss and you may not be able to grasp any solution to the surrounding mess. The pressing question is, "I am divorced, now what?"

Just like a land storm, divorce leaves damage you have to assess in order to rebuild. I learned valuable lessons from both the land storm, Wilma and my Divorce Storm.

I remember how scary it was not knowing what my future would be like. Would I be single and alone for the rest of my life? Would I always struggle financially? Would my children repeat the same cycle of divorce in their own relationships? I had so many questions and sometimes it looked dim.

I am reminded of a sermon I heard one Sunday. Feeling sad about making the decision to file for divorce, I needed encouragement. This message did it.

The story involved a crippled man who wanted to be healed. Sadly, he suffered from his condition for a long time. Jesus approached him and asked, "Do you want to be made whole?" At first, the invalid gave excuses why he never received healing. He told Jesus he had no help getting into the healing pool and when the opportunity came, others got in front of him and were healed instead. What was funny is Jesus did no further talking to him about his situation. It appeared the excuses the man gave went right over His head. What Jesus said next is what stuck in my mind that day. He commanded, "GET UP, take up your bed and walk!" The man did no further explaining or pleading his case. He was obedient. That is when he received his healing. He took up his mat and walked!

That was my motivation to finish the race. It no longer mattered what I had been through, who did what or who was not there. What mattered was that I not let the end of a relationship be my excuse to remain paralyzed and hopeless. I had laid down long enough. I was still in pain but realized it was crucial I got up!

I am saying to you it will take you choosing to do the same. You will have to get up!

I will equip you with a few things to help you toward getting your life put back together. Though things may look catastrophic, just keep in mind if done right, the "Aftermath" stage of your life storm can be a time of reflection that moves you into your final stage of victory.

Let's redirect our attention to what an "aftermath" is. I found something interesting about its meaning. According to the Oxford dictionary, an aftermath is: "the consequences or after effects of a significant unpleasant event". The synonyms include: repercussions, results and (interestingly) fruits. Can you make the connection between the aftermath and what you have experienced because of your divorce?

THE AFTERMATH BEFORE THE DIVORCE

There may have been consequences or repercussions of many unpleasant events that led up to the demise of your marriage. If you have done the self-assessment up to this point, you have already addressed your part in why the marriage met its doom. Now let's be clear. I am not saying it was all your fault. But to say one person in a relationship caused its ending would be misleading. If you allowed certain things, you played a part. Our part rests in the choices we made. Choices to take unfair treatment, to accept disrespect, and to stay when we know we should have been the one to leave the relationship long time ago. You have heard the saying "It takes two." Yes, it really does.

In the "aftermath" definition, the synonym I found interesting was "fruit." Biblically there are verses dealing with fruit. In Galatians 5:19-21, God talks about ungodly fruit such as "sexual immorality, strife, fits of anger, jealousy, envy, drunkenness, rivalry, division, and idolatry." Remember I mentioned saying I may have idolized my husband and my marriage? I strongly believe I did. That was one of my ungodly fruits.

I am not bringing any of this up to condemn but to give insight on the "fruit" that may have played a part in the death of your marriage whether it was you or your ex who contributed to these or others. Perhaps you may have done none of this but allowed it. Is this making sense?

Would you agree with me one of the ungodly fruit both parties in marriages are guilty of is strife of the tongue? Often both are blameworthy of causing separation with their mouths because of the words they spoke and how they spoke them to one another.

In Proverbs 18:21, New Living Translation, says: "The tongue can bring death or life; those who love to talk will reap the consequences". What does that mean? It means you have the power to speak life or death into or over your marriage. Can you admit sometimes you spoke words that had nothing to do with life? It was tongues but not the one you were taught in bible study. Am I right? Our words can cut through steel. We do not recognize the power they have. We may have used that power against our marriage rather than for it. We have all been guilty of it.

I mentioned I prayed for my marriage but looking back, after my own assessment, I made mistakes that may have been detrimental and cancelled out my prayers. I often prayed but turned right around and spoke about the situation I saw in front of me versus the thing I prayed for God to change. In addition, I often prayed in fear rather than in belief. I "hoped" God would change us and save our marriage instead of "believing" He would. There is a big difference. Can you relate?

I know my mouth and the words I spoke in "fits of rage" utterly destroyed my marriage with each argument (that is the part I played in the death of my marriage). I never liked confrontation because I dislike hurting other people's feelings. I'd rather not say anything. But when pushed, there was another side to this little Christian girl that would make the Pastor blush. Can I be real about it? My words were sharp as blades, flowed smooth as water and I did not even have to cuss. This was my way of defending myself if I felt backed into a corner. It was like speaking another language fluently. It took multiple occurrences to get me there because I held a lot of my feelings in but once there I became another person. It felt as if I was stepping outside of myself and I would let him have it! Now mind you, he was no weak opponent and returned the favor. Maybe because I admired his strength, I thought he could take it. What I didn't realize is during those times no matter how tough he appeared to be in my eyes, those words hurt him. Back in the day, it was a way to get his attention. It was even a game of passion; breaking up only to receive an explosive makeup. But that was a worthless and unproductive way to handle a relationship. I realized it was pure unhealthy communication. I did not know how to communicate that he hurt me. Instead it came out in words of anger.

See, death and life are in the power of the tongue; and they that love it shall eat the fruit thereof. That is the King James version; but let me give you one more before I go on. I love the spin the Message Bible puts on this same verse: "*Words kill, words give life; they are either poison or "fruit", you choose*" Wow! How powerful and eye opening is that?

It's sad some of us hate to admit our wrongs in a relationship. We should not be afraid to check ourselves. We need that. In fact, it is freeing when we can accept the truth about ourselves. In order to heal we have to face some real truths; not about our ex but about ourselves. This is about YOU! Remember, the storm has a purpose. Could it be to clean you up and help you grow? Embrace this gift and do not be afraid to learn from your past mistakes!

THE AFTERMATH AFTER THE DIVORCE

Life is unfair and you may have your secret bouts with God. Especially if everything appears to be falling in place for your ex and you are alone and struggling. If you have the kids, you are not only dealing with your own raw emotions, but you must deal with theirs. This can drain your energy. You have made significant strides up to this point but you are experiencing episodes of feeling "stuck" and being overwhelmed. I get it.

I was told to be strong for my kids. *Strong?* Most of the time I barely existed. My mind was in a constant fog. Where would I find this strength? Who would be strong for me because I, Ms. Fix-It, was emotionally done. But with the grace of God, I found it. Although sometimes faking it until I made it, I eventually learned to trust in God's strength and not my own because I had none left. I had to first admit I needed help and that it was ok that I needed it.

Besides, I had to be strong to have survived this storm. I did not end up on drugs, dead or in a strait jacket. For that I give God the glory. I had nothing to do with it.

Strength comes from the willingness to trust God and to go through life lessons instead of running away from them. No matter how painful it may seem, all of what we go through is not in vain. It has our life lessons and the components that make up the part we play in our own life story.

May I be even more honest with you? As I write this book, hell is still breaking loose in my life. Just when I thought I had conquered one thing something else showed up to bring me two steps back. These are what I call the "mini-storms" They happen in the midst of the Divorce Storm.

Something has changed, though. What use to cause extreme panic is now finding me calmer and more resilient. I still have my moments but it is different now. I have a stronger "bounce back" spirit than I had before. I credit it to this experience of divorce.

Two things I want you to realize. First, the storm is almost over but that does not exempt you from life's disappointments. We have an adversary that is real and he will continue to do his job of stealing, killing and destroying. Do your job too! Learn from this experience. Assess the damage and commit to working on rebuilding your life. Identify your opponent's strategy. Recognize your triggers and what he uses to trip you up. You will have to put a plan of action into place to counteract his attack. He knows all about you and it is in your best interest to know about him too.

The second thing I want you to know is being transparent and honest does not make you weak but only strengthens you. So it is ok to admit that you still have moments of despair long after you have overcome a storm in your life. Keep pushing no matter what the aftermath looks like. Keep pushing no matter what else comes your way. It is just a signal that greater things are coming. Nothing lasts forever; good or bad. In this life, we will have various trials and tribulations but we will equally have many triumphs and victories. The circle of life will continue to repeat itself. Picture it, if you're dealing with bad times now, the circle will eventually bring the good, right?

Wow! You have been through the storm. Did you hear that? You have made it through the storm of this divorce. It brewed, it brought with it some high winds and heavy rains, it hit you hard, and there was a moment of peace followed by more devastation. You were left with the rubble of its aftermath but guess what; YOU MADE IT THROUGH! Get excited. Now it's time to rebuild. You have earned it! You are worthy of a great future, if that is what you choose.

Cleaning up the mess looks intimidating, but it is more rewarding than you think. Your perception will be key.

So what can we take from this phase called AFTERMATH? The Aftermath will help us as we move on to the next stage and prepare to tidy up this mess. Let's get busy as we move to the CLEAN UP stage of the storm. You are doing great!

EXPERIENCE OF THE STORM

1. You may be angry!

2. You FINALLY get that it is OVER!

3. You may use your anger to propel forward.

4. You may still have moments when you wonder how life would have been if you had continued the marriage but the moments are short lived.

5. You are more open to reflect on things you were afraid to face about yourself.

6. You want to WIN more than anything!

7. Sometimes you still feel lost or stuck.

8. The mess looks huge and even hopeless but you know you have to live YOUR life.

9. The ups and downs and setbacks hurt but you realize they were necessary.

10. You are learning the lessons the storm teaches you.

11. You go through the final "Life is so unfair" tantrum.

12. You are now ready, in your heart, to accept the changes in your life.

SHELTER-TAKE COVER

1. Stop replaying the lies someone has said about who you are. They are not your creator, God is. Believe what He says, not an imperfect man or woman with issues and flaws of their own.

2. Get passionate about loving yourself. Just like you would for someone you love that was hurting. Do nice things for yourself often. Speak kindly to yourself. For instance, in the morning look in the mirror and say, "Good morning, Beautiful (Handsome for the fellas). Encourage yourself. Tell yourself "I will get through this and I will be stronger because of this."

3. If you are thinking negatively about yourself, work diligently to change that. Make it your life's homework assignment to make the necessary changes. Learn to accept things outside yourself that you cannot change (other people for instance).

4. Trust God's answer whether it is yes or no. If his answer is no, try not to be disappointed. Look for the lesson in this storm. The woulda-shoulda-coulda will not change the fact you are divorced. Stop obsessing over the past. Use that energy to make a better future for yourself.

5. In forgiving, do not forget to forgive yourself. Do not continue to condemn yourself, especially, if you know you did your best to make it work. Remember, we are not responsible for what another person sees or fails to see. What is important is that you see yourself in a new light, work on improving and keep moving forward.

6. Take a self-assessment throughout your life to improve yourself each step of the way. Be your biggest

competitor without putting yourself down. Make competition with yourself fun and reward yourself for each thing you accomplish big and small.

7. Make a list of things you did not like about your relationship with your ex. What things hurt you the most? This exercise is not meant to place blame but to help you to express your feelings, to acknowledge the issues and to help you know what you want and do not want in your next relationship.

8. Now make a list of all the good things you liked about your former relationship. What things attracted you to them in the first place? (It is ok to admit there was good in them).

9. Now make a list of qualities you want in your next relationship. What qualities do you most admire in a mate? What are your "must haves"? What are deal breakers or things you will not accept? Do you possess the same qualities you are requiring from a mate?

10. Perform a "letting go" ritual. Here are a few:

Write a ghost letter telling your ex how you feel about the way things were handled. Get raw with it. Hold nothing back. Please, do not send it to them! Shred the letter or drown it in water in the sink.

Do a scribble a "pretty picture" method shared by one of my sister's /"Trues". Take out two sheets of paper. Draw on the first sheet anything that comes to mind no matter how weird. Do not try to be perfect. Scribble. Mess it up. Poke holes in it! Let your emotions guide you. Next, take the second sheet and draw something pretty. You have released your ugly feelings in the first. It is a reminder that ugly things happened in your life but now you get to recreate something beautiful.

You can use the chair method (since I have a big imagination, I had fun with this one). Pull up a chair and stand in front of it. Talk to the imaginary form of your ex as if you were looking them in the eyes. Just like with the letter, share everything you feel. Make your ex aware of everything on your heart you never had a chance to say. Good and bad. Let him or her know how this made you feel. Forgive your ex-spouse and tell him so. Release him (her). And walk off without looking back.

11. Get actively involved. Give back. Refocusing your attention on helping someone may be exactly what you need. You are helping someone else but they are helping you, too. A win-win for everyone.

12. Word of caution, do not hide in busyness to numb the pain. It will not work. Get involved with a mindset you will help and move forward in your healing.

13. Accept that it's over and it's okay. Stop wanting someone who have made it clear they do not want you. Your worth is not found in their interpretation of you, period. Let it burn, let it soak in and let it go. You do not need them to live. God created you, your ex did not.

14. Face the fact they do not have feelings for you anymore. It has nothing to do with love. "Love" would have never left you.

15. Do not beat yourself up if you still feel you are in love with them. Work through those feelings. Honestly, ask why you feel this way, especially if they have shown you every reason you should let go. Sometimes it has more to do with our inner feelings about ourselves and our fears.

FOOD SUPPLY

1. Life is not always fair but it does not have to be. You can handle it!

2. You are stronger than you give yourself credit for.

3. You matter too.

4. After the bad, the good will show up.

5. There is always hope in what looks hopeless. It's all in how you choose to look at it.

6. You have been through a lot, but guess what, you are still here!

7. You are a beautiful soul worthy of God's best!

WATER-QUENCH YOUR SOUL

Things are tough and you have had to face some harsh realities. The life you knew is no longer the one destined for your future. You realize you want to move on but you may not know how. Everything seems out of order. You have gone through the bad. Goodness is about to show up. Your past is behind. Your future is waiting. Say this prayer:

Lord, what is done is done. Thank you. Life may not seem fair but I realize as long as I have You it does not have to be. I have Your Favor. Thank You that the pain and heartbreak of this storm has provided everything I need to move into the purpose You have for me. You are in control. As long as I trust You, I can be assured things will work out for my good because You love me. Thank You for the lessons this storm has taught me. Thank You for loving and allowing me to go through this storm and bringing me out safe and unharmed. For only You can do this. Thank You, Lord. I did not think I would make it but I have. What was designed to take me out did not. No weapon formed against me could prosper. There have been some losses along this journey but I thank You for the treasures You have allowed me to find. Thank You for being with me the whole time. You never left me. You kept Your promise. From this point on, let me be a tree that produces good fruit. Let this lesson remind me to stay humble, obedient and forever trusting in You. I give You all the praise, honor and glory, Lord. I am ready now. In Jesus name. Amen.

THE CLEAN UP

You fought hard to get here! You survived disappointments, setbacks and pain. But you made it! Now let's get rid of some mess! Time to clean it up!

I will not focus on the land storm here but on cleaning up your life after the Divorce Storm. In this phase, analysis the damage, face some truth and pin-point areas where we may have missed your healing. This stage will provide a treasure chest of information so dig in.

THE BEGININNG OF THE CLEAN UP

My cleanup phase began long before I realized it. I got a call from one of my besties in Florida who said she would be in Atlanta and bought me a ticket to go to the Woman Thou Art Loose Conference 2012. By this time, I had been separated for three months and needed encouragement.

Words cannot describe what that weekend did for my life. My friends and I received favor after favor. Spiritual blessings in droves everywhere we went. I never experienced so many divine encounters at one time in my life. For the first time, I accepted my crown as God's daughter. The woman who was made to hate her smile felt beautiful! It was not the end of the storm but the birth of discovering my worth and my purpose here on this earth.

The road to recovery was long and hard. At first, it was easy to put on my happy smile and do what I had to do. My divorce could not take over my daily life. I was too busy for that. With work, my family, school, church, and all the other activities on my list, I had to stay focused. Crying or hurting had to take a back burner. It gave people a false sense that I was ok with this. And at times, I thought I was. But behind my smile, I was still struggling with this.

I was doing all the right things. Had many hobbies, started school, got a new hairdo, socialized more but my past still had a hold on me. It was not as often but I noticed a pattern. Feelings of fear and insecurities would show up the moment I stepped out to work on improving my life in a major way. Excitement of doing new things was met by crippling moments of rejection. Yes, Dwanese, I see that you have signed up for school but why were you not wanted? Why did he leave? Something must be wrong with you? Those thoughts would come at random times. At first, I could not pinpoint where they were coming from or why. This use to drive me crazy! I was supposed to be over this! Why am I still held ransom over someone else's decision to reject me? I have to get past this! "I am divorced I, get it!" I would shout in frustration.

MY FIRST ASSESSMENT

Because I was so determined to prove to the world that this Divorce Storm did not beat me, I did not realize I was defeating myself. I felt I would only be victorious if I had no feelings for him at all. My cousin who, is also divorced, once told me those feelings of good times you shared never go away but become less painful. I was set to prove her wrong. I wanted them all gone as if they never existed. I'm laughing now because again, it does not work like that. My focus was all wrong. This was not about him. I did not need to fight the feelings I had about my ex or our past together as some badge of honor to prove I had won. My survival already proved it. When I got this part of my assessment, I felt free. So now if my children and I are talking about a great memory we had with him, I am happy to remember and reminisce with them. When I stopped fighting my past and focused on becoming a better me, I began to heal on a far greater level.

MY SECOND ASSESSMENT

I wondered how I was going to get past "the mess". Nothing made it magically happen for me. I had put myself on an unrealistic timetable to be over it. Like I mentioned, I was struggling. "What is the real reason you are holding on, Dwanese?" I asked. There was a reason. I wanted to believe it was because I still loved him but it was much deeper than that. Loving him was not it. I use to think, "If only he would have loved me, we would still be together". But, it was not about his love for me that mattered, it was my own. Things were about to get REAL! I knew it would take some soul searching and hard work to change. And, I was determined to do the work.

He was gone. I was no longer a part of his life's plan. I let that reality hit me and hit me hard. I needed that painful truth to sink into the core of my soul. I needed it to hurt until I accepted its truth! This is the moment I needed to realize the love I wanted did not need to come from him but it had to come from ME for ME. My mind and my heart connected and as painful as it was, I got it!

MY CLEAN UP

I discovered the final piece of the puzzle during this stage of the storm. It was something I truly discovered for myself. I did not get this part from a book or seminar. No well-meaning family member or friend could do this for me. It came to me when I was ready. This ultimate piece of the puzzle had less to do with the best advice I received and more to do with my mindset and my heart. It had to be something I made up in my mind to do.

All this time, I felt I had lost my best friend. But I knew if I was going to save my real best friend, I had to be willing to let go of everything that would destroy her well-being. I discovered my real best friend was me and she needed me to get my act together. I started being a better friend to myself. I finally understood in order to love others genuinely I had to love myself first. Look at what the bible says, "Love others as though you love yourself." How can any of us effectively love others when most of us have not really discovered how to love ourselves? "Could this be why there are so many failed marriages?

Upon getting that revelation, I knew I was on to something. That was the beginning of my self-love journey. I started to treat myself like I would treat my most loved friend. I took myself out on dinner dates, parked my car and listened to the radio at night while watching the stars. On sunny days, I watched the trees blow in the wind and admired the splendor of nature. I intentionally noticed how beautifully God painted the sky and the flowers. It became addictive. I gravitated to the very things that soothed my soul and brought peace to my spirit. I was on the right track.

I'm amazed at how much I have learned about myself and my faith. If it had not been for the Divorce, I would have continued to live like I had it spiritually together. I was stretched beyond limits I did not think I could go. The closer I got to God, the more He revealed. That was the whole point. God used my adversities to clean me up and under the mess I discovered Dwanese. My "authentic" me.

She was smart, she was creative. She was funny and had a heart of gold that was hidden in mistrust and pain. She wore a crown and knew she was Royalty. Her Daddy told her that! And I loved her. She was the "me" I always wanted to be but was locked away by another person's lack of value for her. The storm came to allow me to find her. And I am so glad I did! But it wasn't easy. I did not find her until I was ready to do the work. I had to accept that my life was a mess and I needed help to clean it up!

YOUR ASSESSMENT

You are wearing a beautiful smile and it looks good on you. It even looks convincing but you are still breaking inside and you do not know why. You are doing some amazing things and have made equally awesome changes. You want badly to be over this. But you are still hurting over the loss of your marriage. It's frustrating! I understand. Our expectations to be completely over the drama of divorce cripples us. You will still have the memories of your former marriage. Fighting against it won't work.

Getting out of your shell and taking all the right steps to move on is fantastic. But if you miss "the Clean Up" all those things become useless. That's why we struggle with letting go of someone who is already living fine without us. We feel ashamed because we are still feeling hopeless. "What would people think if they knew I still had moments when I am weak?" you ask. The truth is recovery is a process so you should not feel embarrassed.

Often we forfeit the process because we are so glad it is over. We rush to get on with our lives. But there is junk left behind by the storm and hidden things we never dealt with. Whatever we fail to deal with now will continue to show up in our lives at inopportune times. To overcome any challenge, we will have to face them. This is no different.

You can get a new haircut, repeat positive affirmations or sign up to run a marathon but until you fully involve your mind and your heart, nothing may change. At least not permanently. It will take a determined mind and heart to get out of this pit. You will have to give all of the focus you have been putting on your ex to someone who really deserves all of it, YOU! That is the secret ingredient to getting over the pain of Divorce. "That's too simple," you may say, but it works.

This is why the "Clean Up" Stage is so important. Here we clean up the debris left by the storm and uncover those hidden things. The things the enemy wants to keep quiet so he can use them at random times to make us feel unworthy.

THE BEGINNING OF YOUR CLEANUP

What is your REAL reason for wanting to hold on? If you are honest with yourself it probably has less to do with your ex and more to do with how you feel about yourself. Nothing to be ashamed of. Even the most confident person can lose themselves during a storm of life. Here, you will make some beautiful changes that will get you to focus and love you more.

Be prepared. Some people may not like the changes you are about to make. They may fear the "authentic" you. But you should be over people's opinions by now. Baby, this is about you and I am so happy for the beautiful YOU that you are about to meet!

With all that being said, do you know this is the most exciting part of the storm? It may not be the easiest though if you are still resisting change. Are you willing to let go now? Can you put down your past, focus on your present and strategize for your future?

Please don't keep hurting yourself by holding on to what was or wished it could be. I ask you to be a little selfish and focus on you right now. The clean up can be the scariest stage of your life because you have to face some hard truths about yourself. You have been so comfortable in your chaos. But it's time to create your new life!

Be warned, this phase of new living is a choice. You have the choice to stay dirty and live in your mess. You even have the right to continue to feel sorry for yourself and feed off the sympathy of others. You can continue to wear the "He Hurt Me" medal of honor while your ex lives happily without you…OR….

You can get your butt up and realize you and God are all you need! Clean yourself up (not just on the outside). I am talking about cleaning up your mind and the way you see yourself and your circumstances. Yes, you are divorced now GET UP! You are still here and life is still yours! Here are a few things I want you to try:

Imagine putting your past in a nice little box, handing it to God and not looking for it to be returned. Maybe the box contained some good memories too but trust God for bigger and better ones. You have been given another chance at a new life.

Get somewhere right now where you can relax. Do this exercise with me. If you did not get a chance to do it before, help your ex, spiritually, pack their bags and escort them to the door. Close your eyes and visualize you helping them put their clothes in the suitcase, letting them out and shutting the door behind them! No longer allow him or her to take up space in your mind or your heart. They are gone in the physical. Now you must allow your heart to let them go emotionally and spiritually. This is the time to get radical about your come back! Thank him or her for leaving and giving you both a chance at something new. A real chance to discover your authentic selves and a new found happiness.

YOUR CLEAN UP

This phase will take some boldness. It will cut against the grain and may not feel good at first. You will be required to be totally honest about things you may not want to face or tried to hide. Get in your own face and demand honesty. Time to clean house!

On the fun side and once you have gotten real, you will get to play dress up and dream again just like when you were a kid. This time you will hold the key to making all your dreams come true and live in the reality of them. Just like God intended for you to do.

In this phase called THE CLEAN UP it is going to take you having a laser focus and a "get up" plan to get you back on track. No more tears over this old stuff. It is time to pick your crown back up Queen! It is time to get back on your thrown King! He or she did not make you and they have no authority to break you. You will only remain in a broken state by choice. It is not their choice to make, it is yours! Mindset matters. You have to clean up your thinking.

I AM SO PROUD OF YOU!! YOU MADE IT THROUGH!

Come, let's start having some fun and clean up this mess!!

EXPERIENCE OF THE STORM

1. You made it!

2. It stings but it does not hurt like it did in the beginning.

3. You have learned so much and have grown tremendously.

4. You may have tried a lot of positive things to improve but still feel like something is missing.

5. You realize the answer lies in YOU to get unstuck.

6. You realize you cannot be lazy about your comeback.

7. You realize you have to put together a "get up" plan.

SHELTER-TAKE COVER

1. Create a plan for your "get up". Yes, this will take you physically and spiritually doing something to get your life back on track. Make a vision board, create a life binder (see Pintrest) or buy a nice notebook and start journaling. Write how you want the next few years of your life to be. Write down things you would like to do now that you have a second chance and a new start. The creator in me loves pictures and helps me to visually see my future. Be as creative as you want to be. Add things to motivate you; pictures, favorite quotes, scriptures, colors, etc.

2. Learn to control your emotions in every aspect of your life. Too many times our emotions get us in trouble. We act and say things we may later regret. Like the bible says, "Be slow to anger and speak and quick to listen". Stay focused and alert at all times. When you become the master of your emotions, you can win the game of life. This does not mean you become hard and unfeeling. It means you become more aware of yourself and things around you without reacting but responding in more positive ways. Ponder over things. Everything does not have to be addressed right away.

3. Be radical about breaking barriers. Make a list of things you would like to do but have been afraid to do. Set a goal to do each one on your list. Fear will show up. Face the fear. Fear is not part of your DNA. It has no legal rights to you. Treat it as an unwanted guest that cannot stay in your house. You do not have time to entertain fear. You have work to do.

4. Get organized (if you are not an organized individual). You cannot operate in chaos no matter how hard you try or think you are in control of things.

5. Especially helpful are lists of all kinds. It was a practice passed on to me as a little girl by both my parents and has helped throughout my life. Lists have saved my life when I was going through the foggiest times. Times when I could not think clearly and felt overwhelmed. Organize your home, your car, your files, your clothes, your office, and your finances. Get help if you need it. You will be able to see where you are at in life and ease unnecessary stress. It frees up time to allow you to focus on you. Get cleaned up! It will have such great rewards.

6. Put the focus on YOU. It is time to get it together. Treat yourself like the royalty you are.

7. Date yourself for a while. Wine and dine yourself. Lavish yourself with compliments. Do not always rely on others to encourage you. Encourage yourself. Be your own best friend and enjoy your company. If you do not like being with you, why would you expect others to? You are all that and then some! Realize it! Own it!

8. Be intentional about your recovery. No longer leave your life to chance. Passionately fight for your recovery. Take every necessary step to get back your joy; YOUR life.

9. Take breaks or hiatuses where you shut out the outside noise but no hiding out. It is ok to keep certain things private. I understand and respect that. In fact I encourage it. What I am talking about is not running away or hiding out because of shame and guilt or any reason that degrades your worth. Let your light shine. Open yourself up to those you love being around and that love being around you. Step out and make new friends, alliances and connections. I am telling you what I know. Secrets and hiding are the breeding ground for lies, disillusions and deception. Besides you have nothing to hide. You get to custom design your world. You get to

choose to surround yourself in love and people who celebrate you.

10. Expect something good to happen for you. If you cannot see good things coming to you, they never will show up. What it looks like now is temporal. Show up on the playing field everyday ready to win. Show up with a spirit of expectancy. Good will come when you open yourself up to receive it. Remember you will attract what you focus on good or bad.

FOOD SUPPLY

1. What was meant to take you out DID NOT WIN!

2. The devil may have gloated but it is you who gets the last laugh. Can you shout VICTORY!!

3. The Storm of Divorce came to destroy you but what you are equipped with on the inside is designed to build you up again.

4. You will recover everything that has been stolen from you. It is a promise!

5. This whole experience is not a total loss, it's your "gold mine" and the hidden treasure is YOU.

6. You have connected with a friend who needs and wants you right now, YOU!

WATER - QUENCH YOUR SOUL

At this moment in your life you should be ready to take on the world. You have learned so much and have bravely stood against the harsh winds of the storm. The smell of victory surrounds you! Take charge of your destiny! You made it out! CONGRATULATIONS! Say this prayer:

Lord, thank You that my story is not over! Reveal to me everything I need to do to get back to living whole as You have intended for me to live all along. Help me to be good to myself. Help me to love myself so that I can properly love others. Show me how You see me. Your Word says I am fearfully and wonderfully made. Make that real for me. Allow me to know in my heart I matter. Clean me up Lord and make me ready to step into every good thing You have for me going forward. Thank You for restoring joy back into my life. Thank You for the hidden treasures You have allowed me to discover along this journey and for the ones yet to be revealed. Thanks for giving me my power back! Victory is mine! In Jesus Name. AMEN.

THE NEXT ONE

I hope you do not think life will be roses because you survived the storm of divorce? You may feel accomplished now because you have gotten over your ex. You may have even met someone new and moved on. That is fantastic news and I am so happy for you! If you are happier now, this is exactly where you should be. However, remember the cycle of life; the good and bad. It is continuous and life does not stop its natural ebb and flow because we find ourselves in a better place.

MY NEXT ONE

I went through the storm of divorce and I survived! My social life was exciting! For a long time I ran from the idea of dating but I was curious. What I did not realize was I would be tested on everything I had just learned in my storm.

You have heard it said the devil does not come dressed in horns with a pit fork but packaged in what you most desire. And it's as if he knew what I wanted. It came packaged in the right color, the right status and all the right words. He was smart, funny, valued communication and very attentive. He recognized I worked hard and wanted to lighten my load. I did not want his money though. I loved the fact he wanted to spend time with me. A little attention was more than enough. I was not searching, but was it possible I was about to receive an unexpected blessing? The blessing was not the kind I expected and almost landed me in another potential storm.

I made a commitment to God. There would be no intimate involvement outside of marriage. Self-control was never a problem for me. I was a military wife. Being abstinent was not an issue for me. I wore my faithfulness like a badge of honor.

So why I was suddenly caught up in feelings I could not understand?

I was ready to give up everything I believed in because I was tired of being good. Besides, look where it got me. Because I was getting something I did not have in a long time, I was willing to risk my walk with God. This felt right, but it wasn't.

In the middle of conversations with friends, I would think about him. Like some teenager with a crush, I would take the long way home just to pass the street where he lived. I felt caught up, and I did not care. My soul felt tied to his. I craved the feeling being with him gave me, but at what cost?

Without realizing it, I had developed a soul tie with this man. Like most women who have been abandoned, I needed validation that I was still attractive. I needed to feel wanted and special. My wish to have a man in my life nearly cost the blessings and rewards God had for me. I almost missed the mark.

The problem was I denied and dismissed what I was feeling because I felt a woman who loved God should not feel that way. I was dismissing something that was a natural part of being a woman and feeling guilty about it because of my faith. You see it all the time. Women who professed to love God and appear to be keeping themselves holy but are miserable and depressed. They feel something is wrong with them for desiring the touch of a man. Let me free some of you. Acknowledge those desires. You are a woman. Hiding those feelings are dangerous. It leave the door open to sin. You do not have to act on those desires, but do not condemn yourself because of them. Expose what you feel so you will not live with hidden guilt and shame. This is a strategic plan of the enemy, and a slick one, I have to admit. He will use it to guilt trip you into giving in to something you know in your heart is not good for you.

I collected myself once I got passed the guilt of those feelings. I asked God for forgiveness because He showed me that is not what He planned for my life. What He had was better than anything I could get from a man.

I did what seemed so hard and cut all ties. No more visits, no phones calls, and no texts. I turned my attention back to my purpose and been moving forward ever since.

What was revealed to me is I wasn't dealing with "the man". It was a spirit that wanted to bring me back to the familiar, dark place I was delivered from. The horns and pitchfork in the spirit realm seeped into my realm and what I saw woke me up before it was too late.

I was volunteering to join the ranks of women who were long-term girlfriends of men who never intended to make them wives. I was about to settle for being someone's arm candy when he needed a woman just for the moment. I risked being a toy for a man to play with and satisfy his manly needs. That's not what God planned for me. And that is not what I wanted for myself.

He was content being a single man. It was no problem giving me what I wanted to get what he wanted. Had I not learned from the divorce storm, I would have been ok with all of that. It was not that I loved him because I did not. I did not know him that well. It was selfish when I think about it. It was also based on fear. I did not want to become the lonely old lady who never got married again. My fear of not being able to know the touch of another man was huge. But if nothing else I learned from the storm of divorce, I learned that no void can replace the love of God and the love a woman should have for herself. When a woman loves herself and knows who she is, her choices will be different. She will evaluate what's right for her and not just what feels good.

This may be confusing for women who have not taken the time to love themselves. We feel something is wrong with us if a man does not love us. This is why I say it's important to love yourself. You run the risk of experiencing more hurt if your expectations differ from the other person. The probability of being a long-time girlfriend instead of a wife increases. You feel your clock is ticking, but he has all the time in the world.

Ladies, we have to respect a man in whatever place he is in. We cannot force them to want to be in a committed relationship he does not want or is ready for. Put that energy into one who is. A man would not be in the wrong if YOU expected something different from him when he has made it clear he is happy with his life without a serious relationship. If you enter, then it's at your own risk. I have to keep it real!

And guys, you are excited to be single again, after coming out of a long-term relationship that has ended. You may not want to be alone and may have many women to pick from. Keep in mind, there are a lot of broken women. Some are recovering from horrible situations. They have to be strong because they are taking care of their children and sometimes ill and aging parents in addition to working. It can be stressful and hard. They may look for genuine love from you. I am not bashing anyone. Just be honest of intentions upfront. It's ok to be honest. Most of us can handle that. We even respect that. Give a woman the choice to be in a relationship with you once you have stated your intentions.

I believe in sowing and reaping and if both men and women are giving each other mutual respect, it will come back to them eventually. Before we commit ourselves to yet another person and in order to have healthy relationships, women and men need to do some soul searching. We have some work to do, don't you agree?

I am not being negative. But you and I both know we have a tendency to forget. We can repeat the same storm over if we have not been careful to pay attention to all we have learned. Wouldn't it be a shame to repeat what you have just been delivered from all because you forgot what you have learned? This is especially true if you rushed the healing process just so you could get on with your life.

Do not think so? Studies have shown that 50% of first marriages end in divorce. I am sure you have heard that. It's probably old news to you since the majority of people you interact with daily are divorced. Alarming to me was the fact that those numbers increase with each number of marriages. Statistics state second marriages have a 67% chance of failing while third marriages have a 73% failure rate! Ask yourself why that is the case. Well somewhere someone forgot what their first life storm taught them. They simply threw caution to the wind and went into the next relationship as if they learned nothing from the previous.

Those facts are disheartening, but you can be among those whose second marriage is successful. It will first take honest evaluation of your life before moving into another committed relationship.

Some of us just do not get that having another person in our lives do not complete us. We have to master ourselves so we will be capable of being in a healthy relationship. You will have to make sure that anyone you enter into a commitment with has done their own self-mastery.

It's ok to be alone for a while so you can work on you. I know to some of you it may seem like you have just received a death sentence. You cannot fathom being alone for a minute. However, the reality is we first have to enjoy spending time and loving ourselves. Yes, I am preaching self-love and self-WORK because I am so proud of the progress you have made. If you have seriously been applying the principles found in this book, you are thriving.

You have been through a huge ordeal and are worth ever second spent reflecting and embracing who you are.

Yes you have made it through this storm but please do not forget the lessons it has taught you. The Divorce Storm served its purpose. It's given you keys to success and personal growth.

Remember I said I found something interesting about the meaning of aftermath? Fruit wasn't the only thing I was referring to. Aftermath also had a second meaning that seemed far-fetched from the meaning as we know it. But here's what I found.

The second meaning relates to farming. In fact, the word is of German origin and its word combination means "after (after) + mowing (math)" or new grass growing after mowing or harvest. This is not saying the grass is greener on the other side. It is the opposite. The definition has nothing to do with finding "new grass" on someone else's turf but it has to do with your own grass; your own life.

It got me thinking, the divorce may have mowed or cut you down to nothing but it only made way for a new harvest to show up in YOUR life. What was cut down, withered and died cleared a path for what is growing, fresh and alive. This is an opportunity for a new harvest.

Yes, there is something to learn even in the aftermath of a storm. Just do not forget what the storm has taught you. It will help you to prepare for the next storm that may come your way.

This is not only true for romantic relationships. It applies to preparing for other life storms such as financial losses, the ending of friendships, loss of loved ones to death, disabilities or failing health or whatever storm comes your way.

What will your survival plan be next time?

EXPERIENCE OF THE STORM

1. You must know trials and tribulations do not end here.

2. You are one level stronger and wiser now.

3. Remember all this storm has taught you.

4. You realize you cannot haphazardly live life; you must plan for life ahead.

5. Another storm can happen at any time.

6. You have the potential to repeat past mistakes in new relationships.

SHELTER - TAKE COVER

1. Other storms will come so prepare for them. Do not be afraid to face issues head on. Do not be afraid to go through life's storms. Take it as an opportunity to learn and grow instead of something to avoid.

2. Do not be afraid to be uncomfortable. This is a time to be stretched beyond your comfort zone.

3. Remember all of the previous storms you have triumphed over. There was a time during the storm you did not think you would overcome it but you did.

4. Do not ignore red flags. Trust your intuition. It will never steer you wrong. What does not look right or feel right probably isn't. Do not rationalize what you know in your gut is wrong. Especially when dealing with new relationships. Do not be afraid to let go if it isn't right.

5. Apply your lessons to the new storm and look for new lessons to learn from also. Always be on the mission of learning.

6. Realize life is not a destination but a continuous journey filled with new adventures, new lessons and new possibilities. Never get to one place and feel you have arrived.

7. Always cover yourself in prayer. Pray without ceasing. It serves as a reserve later for things you may face along the way.

8. Always remember to be humble and grateful. Never think of yourself too great that you cannot fall. Be grateful for the life God has given you even in the good and bad times. Live, baby, LIVE!

FOOD SUPPLY

1. You have earned your right to be called a "Survivor"!

2. You have gained experiences embedded in your being which will prepare you for other life storms that come your way.

3. Strength, knowledge, self-love and wisdom are all yours for making it through what you thought defeated you.

4. You are not the same. You were determined and now you have won!

5. Life is full of lessons and is a continuous journey. Use what you have learned to unlocked the door to your greatest life yet.

WATER - QUENCH YOUR SOUL

Life appears good again. But, do not take your focus off the One who has brought you through. It is easy to lose focus and forget once you live in the light of day again. Remember God, the storm and all the lessons you have learned to help you for other life challenges you may face ahead. They are coming. Be prepared this time! Say this prayer:

Lord, I have been through so much and You have brought me through it all. Do not take Your hands off of me. Do not let me forget the reason for the storm and all it has taught me. Give me strategic plans to conquer anything that may come against me in my future. Let me remember Your faithfulness when things may occasionally get hard. You are my rock and my fortress. I thank You, Lord that you have given me Your full armor to protect me against my enemies. Remind me every time I forget to put it on. Let me not fail to realize the importance of what my armor is designed to do. What the enemy meant for my harm it has certainly turned out for my good. I made it Lord and with You, victory will always be mine. In Jesus Name, Amen.

HELP AND ENCOURAGEMENT

Trust	and	Faith
Jeremiah 29:11		2 Corinthians 5:7
Psalm 84:11-12		Proverbs 3:5-6
James 1:2-4		

Strength	and	Healing of Broken Heart
2 Corinthians 12:10		Psalm 147:3
Philippians 4:12-13		

Protection	and	Comfort
Psalm 91:1-6		Deuteronomy 31:6
Isaiah 54:15-17		

Forgiveness	and	God's Vengeance
Matthew 5:44-47		Romans 12:19-21
Matthew 6:12		Deuteronomy 32:35-36

"Weeping may endure for a night but joy comes in the morning"
~Psalm 30:5

NOTES

"Aftermath - Definition of Aftermath in English | Oxford Dictionaries." Oxford Dictionaries.
https://en.oxforddictionaries.com/definition/aftermath

"Storm - Definition of Storm in English | Oxford Dictionaries." Oxford Dictionaries.
https://en.oxforddictionaries.com/definition/storm

By Age 40 I Realized We Were Talking past Each Other and Took the Hard Decision to Split. Best Thing I Ever Did. "Divorce Statistics and Divorce Rate in the USA." Divorce Statistics Comments. http://www.divorcestatistics.info/divorce-statistics-and-divorce-rate-in-the-usa.html

AFTER THE LOVE HAS GONE: SURVIVING THE 8 STAGES OF A DIVORCE STORM

MAKE SURE YOU CONNECT WITH ME!

Join the community at Dwanese E Love on Facebook and follow @DwaneseELove on Twitter and @dwaneseelove on Instagram and Snapchat